108 Quotations

A Treasury of Mystical Wisdom

By the Venerable Dhyani Ywahoo

Copyright © 2012 The Venerable Dhyani Ywahoo
All rights reserved.

ISBN-13: 978-1468001396
ISBN-10: 1468001396

IN APPRECIATION

To these wise women who have encouraged me to share these teachings.

Aunt Leala, sister of my Grandmother.

My Grandmother Nellie and her city husband, John, with me and my sister Pam.

My maternal Grandfather and my two oldest daughters.

A special thanks to Shan Watters and Emily Corey for encouraging me to pass along these teachings.

DEDICATION

May the readers of this book realize this is a stream and everyone is a part of it. The short quotations are excerpts from longer teachings. May they be a mirror and an echo of the wisdom potential within your own life.

~ The Venerable Dhyani Ywahoo

Oh, Mother of Wisdom, our offerings are made,
Oh, Mother of Wisdom, supplication is made,
We embody your wisdom light.

Oh, Father of Action, our offerings are made,
Oh, Father of Action, supplication is made,
We embody your skillful means.

Oh, Child of Bliss, our offerings are made,
Oh, Child of Bliss, supplication is made,
We embody your joyful light.

SKYWALKER TEACHINGS
A Song of Prayer

Prayer is part of a dynamic relationship with the environment. The ceremonies of appreciation and healing are to augment and complete the flow of blessings that already exist. You don't have to go anywhere to get the blessings. They are here. It is just a matter of resonating with them.

MEDICINE WHEEL MANDALA TEACHINGS

Love is a sacred medicine.

VAJRA DAKINI TEACHINGS

The ascending wind arises from the potential of space and in and of itself, is wisdom and potential. In the human body, this ascending wind meets with the descending breeze of skill, thereby creating a vortex through which one's potential may be expressed. The descending wind you think of as the Sky Father, Heavenly Father, and through that dynamic interaction of Mother and Father, worlds are born.

THE SEVEN WINDS

In considering all those who have been our Mothers, it becomes clear that we are relatives and the energy of the Mother is inseparable from wisdom. By recognizing this, we recognize direct, awakened understanding.

CRYSTAL TEACHINGS

*In Native American tradition,
you don't pray for anything;
you pray to give thanks.*

MEDICINE WHEEL MANDALA

The memory that we have all arisen from one light is to reweave the tapestry of stable, wholesome relationships, or simply put, a tapestry of beauty. This view indicates that individuals are a part of this dream and each individual's responses create new fields of potential and opportunity.

LEARNING CHEROKEE WAYS

Seeing the bounty and ease within and all around, and diligently fanning the flame of certainty, opens the channel for dissonance to resolve naturally into harmony.

VOICES OF OUR ANCESTORS

Transformation is a reciprocal dance.

GADUGI TEACHINGS

By energizing yourself as a wisdom
being you are quickening and magnetizing
that seed of wisdom potential within yourself
and clarifying the pathways so wisdom
may become skillful activity.

CRYSTAL TEACHINGS

Father-Mother wisdom is our natural state.

GADUGI TEACHINGS 2011

When sadness or illness arises, often it is because one has become out of tune. The basis of our healing tradition is to re-tune one's organ systems and thought patterns so that one may resonate in harmony with the pulse beat of the earth and sky, thus inviting wisdom to appear.

LEARNING CHEROKEE WAYS

A lot of learning as children
was related to our observation of the trees.
In this observation, we learned to inhale the
earth and exhale the sky, inhale the sky, and
exhale the earth. Think of oneself as a living
being that receives and offers in the circle
of life. Inhale the earth, exhale the sky,
inhale the sky and exhale the earth.
See what one notices.

LEARNING CHEROKEE WAYS

Everyone has power, because everyone is a dynamic living form.

TEACHING OF THE TREES

We do not do ceremonies because of a cultural view. We do ceremonies because our lives depend upon it.

MEDICINE WHEEL MANDALA

The group mind of earth has been disturbed through grasping ignorance, through pushing away, thinking others are not worthy, through selfishness, through wanting to control. This has disturbed that network of light and it is our time, our choice, to re-energize the fabric of compassion. Whatever is the experience, allow that information to flow to the source in that it is all a dance of exploration.

CRYSTAL TEACHINGS

Human beings are a bridge to what arises. It is through the element of water and the understanding that water is wisdom, that we may invite ourselves to grow and recall our original state and return the pulse of the wisdom of our exploration to the very field from whence we have all arisen.

WATER PRACTICE TEACHINGS

*You cannot abdicate the responsibility
of your holiness.*

VOICES OF OUR ANCESTORS

When we weave the dream together,
and the more we appreciate the dance of
the cells that make our bodies—the earth,
the stars, and the light itself—the clearer it
is that we have never been separated
from that original state of one light.

LEARNING CHEROKEE WAYS

When we consciously take note
and give thanks for what we receive,
there is a completion of the circuit.
Much suffering comes from
not realizing what we receive.

MEDICINE WHEEL MANDALA

———

The Red Cardinal is the translator of the forest history. Even today, I find this experience continues. When I visit sacred areas anywhere in the world, great eagles appear, usually a pair. For example, when one enters Hopi in the right way, when one approaches the area with good heart and makes prayers and offerings, two eagles come and circle above, almost like escorts.

LEARNING CHEROKEE WAYS

The Dance increased our ability to sense through our hands. Inhaling, we held our hands over an object, like a stone, and read its message. This was taught so we would recognize the impressions left in the environment from others who passed by. This reminded us that our thought, word, and action left ripples in the field of light.

THE SEVEN WINDS

———

*C*eremony is essential for survival. Our lives depend upon it. I was taught that ceremonies are part of the circle of life and that we each have a spiritual responsibility to contribute to the cycles of creation. Our thoughts, words, and actions contribute to the state of our communities, families, planet, and universe. Prayers spoken were and are those of thanksgiving and appreciation.

LEARNING CHEROKEE WAYS

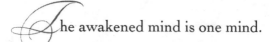he awakened mind is one mind.

MEDICINE WHEEL MANDALA

The earth and the sun are having
an incredible conversation from the deepness
of space; and from beyond what is known are
coming waves of energy. These waves of energy
are to impel us into the remembrance that we are
spiritual beings learning to be human, learning
about matter. May the wisdom potential
in each person flourish and grow.

May the glory that flows through the universe
and the blessings that move through each
of us, bring forth ever more skillful methods
of activity. The earth is alive and we are in the
womb of her atmosphere continuously being
reborn through the grace of the heavens.

MASTERFUL LIVING

Just to practice appreciation with our food and our water is healing the circle of good relationship and actually creates a network through which we may connect and re-weave the circle of life.

MEDICINE WHEEL MANDALA

*E*xperience the earth's crust like skin, bones, and clothing. Experience the earth and sky as energy in which you have a relationship. There is a certain point where you realize you are inseparable from earth's perspective, and sense how it feels that people have forgotten the cycle of reciprocity. Sense how unkind actions affect the earth and how skillful, kind actions return positive energy to the pulse of the earth.

MEDICINE WHEEL MANDALA

We give thanks by acknowledging
all the gifts that are continually showered
upon us through the dance of the universe.
Giving thanks to the air, earth, water,
and fire we understand and we
continuously receive blessings.
How wonderful.

LEARNING CHEROKEE WAYS

Behind the sun, her brother comes out from hiding. That sun behind the sun is another dimension that our consciousness is moving toward.

MEDICINE WHEEL MANDALA

When we are aware of our circle breath and that we are light and space, we become cognizant of the etheric web that allows us to tune in and relate to all beings that resonate with the pulse of life. This primary pulse comes from the center of the universe. It is like a pipe organ that has a pedal tone that holds the song together. The earth herself has a pulse and all who share in her dream of life resonate with her pulse through the center of our brains. In this way, we are all connected.

LEARNING CHEROKEE WAYS

All beings are connected through an underlying fabric, which is described by many Medicine Elders as a pulsing crystal plate supported by four cords in the vastness. This pulsing crystal plate, and its undulations, gives rise to overtones of matter and individualized states of consciousness. This plate is the primary tone and as it vibrates, it gives rise to myriad frequencies, which become the basis of matter.

LEARNING CHEROKEE WAYS

Remember that all beings are
your relatives. Energize the falling away
of discordant thought and actions
and replace them with thoughts of
appreciation and reconciliation.

MEDICINE WHEEL MANDALA

As we moved through the forest, from the corner of my eyes I could see sparkling villages of light. I understood then, that this was more than a story. Our people had indeed vibrated into another realm. My childlike mind thought, I too vibrate in many realms.

LEARNING CHEROKEE WAYS

𝓔ach and every one of us can be someone's angel. When we look at another human being, we see their luminous potential and recognize that this human being has within them the seed of most perfect mind.

CRYSTAL TEACHINGS

———

By recognizing that each element has a relationship to our emotions and supports our physical body, and that through the transformation of these emotions into their inherent awakened state, we are putting the weapons that cause suffering at the roots of the Tree of Peace.

WATER PRACTICE TEACHINGS

It is a brave human being who is
able to make amends.

MASTERFUL LIVING

Ceremony is the opportunity to say thank you. It is the gift of our life force and our thought to explore the potential. Ceremony honors the cycles of the moon, the sun, and even more subtle cycles that connect our solar system with other galaxies and the very heart of this and all universes.

LEARNING CHEROKEE WAYS

From the One we have come and to the One we are returning. Just within the single body that you sit in at this moment, there are many beings, your cells, and your potential. To be in touch with all those beings, and to express harmoniously the wisdom of the many within the One, that is to be integrated, that is to blaze forth in glory.

VOICES OF OUR ANCESTORS

The Little People's voices are beautifully melodic and when they sing together, it is like the sound of fine glass bells. Their drumbeat is very, very fast when they play their water drums. They are renowned for their understanding of healing herbs and share that wisdom with those who ask. A water drum is a powerful medicine object carved from a tree and then hollowed out. The bottom is solid wood and the drum is covered with a skin and filled with water. One coaxes pulses of the universe from the vibration of the drum and water.

LEARNING CHEROKEE WAYS

Far away in the realm of Galunlati, the Seventh Heaven, there are crystal beings singing. Their songs give order to chaos. They sing for all who would hear, of worlds in harmony.

VOICES OF OUR ANCESTORS

To recognize our home in the stars is to prepare all nations upon this planet for a leap into the realization of our universal relationship.

VOICES OF OUR ANCESTORS

Magnetization is a principle of attraction. By our patterns of thought, we attract to our life circle that which appears. Through the generation of sound power, prayer power, a harmonious relationship with the sacred law, we can attract what will benefit all. Our days arise out of our mind's actions, where one is conscious of the patterns of attraction and repulsion or not. It is incumbent upon each human being who wishes to live in a sacred manner to maintain a spiritual practice and a moral and ethical framework of living.

THE SEVEN WINDS

In Tibetan medicine there is something like a vein, a channel near the heart where the karmic residue is stored. Over time, and through pacifying, purifying, and energizing the seeds of wisdom within, it becomes empty. Then one places their attention on the awakened beings who have demonstrated awakened mind.

MASTERFUL LIVING

In this moment we energize the apperances of tomorrow and transform the past.

WISDOM STREAMS FROM THE SKY

Just as energy comes from the quasar, spiraling disks of energy and a blue-white jet, that same emblem can be perceived in our own hearts. Spiraling energy of galaxies from whence a blue-white jet emerges reminds us that we are continually in a dance of creation. Our bones vibrate with the pulse of the earth and sky. Our mind, our being, is energized by the lightening grid work of the earth. All appearances are vibration and what we choose to view is what we see, yet beyond the usual appearances, there are amazing displays of our perfection.

The potential is what impels us to explore and understand what is the nature of mind? What is the reason that one has taken birth? Why have we chosen to explore this field of potential and how is it we land upon the earth? She too is a living being and is expanding, and in a sense, we are part of her evolution. She is now growing just as our consciousness is growing. Like a song changing key, we are moving into a new dimension.

MASTERFUL LIVING

The One Who Thinks the Breath Creates is how Creator is expressed in some of the old Tsalagi hymns. The breath carries thought around the world. Through mindfulness of the breath mental errors are transformed. The bellows fan the wisdom fire. Wise person, take care, for your thoughts, words, deeds today, blow clouds across the sky of tomorrow.

VOICES OF OUR ANCESTORS

Caring for the fire is caring for
the wisdom seed in every being.

TEACHING OF THE TREES

All physical form — the man made objects we see, the trees and flowers, the mountains — was first a thought. Some thoughts originate in the mind of God, some originate in the minds of the people. All thought is united in the Sacred Hoop, in that we are one in Creation. If we refer to this inclusiveness of mind as Buddha-mind, Christ-mind, Great Spirit, Allah, essentially there is one truth underlying our attempts to describe what is indescribable.

THE SEVEN WINDS

Consciousness is aware of
our multidimensionality.

MASTERFUL LIVING

From the early experiments at Brookhaven National Laboratories it became apparent that by observing an electron's trajectory, one actually changed it. There were some waves, some energy, that moved from the eye and had an impact upon the trajectory of the electrons as they left the outer electron ring. That was a first indication that our minds have an impact, or that there is some sort of carrier wave that will carry our thought, our intention, and even the way we are observing the world. This is carried and has an affect on other elements in the dance. So, from the Native American perspective this reminds us of the importance of cultivating a view and understanding that every human being is in the process of continually growing and revealing that inherent wisdom state, and that we have never separated from it.

TIME TRAVEL TEACHINGS

The same awareness of form that a child has, knowing the form from within, is what we are reaching for. Learning to speak true, to affirm our vision, is just a recognition of certain patterns, certain sounds, certain realities. We can choose to be in a certain part of the wave or even attuned to a particular frequency and maintain an area of illuminated consciousness within that space. This means understanding vibration and realizing that there is in every aspect of life, a cycle, a process. It is by being attuned to the larger cycle in the sacred wheel that we draw ourselves and our environment more and more into harmony.

VOICES OF OUR ANCESTORS

So that we may move harmoniously with the natural awakened state and that we may perceive the universe as vibrating energy, let us first take note of the vibrating energy within ourselves, and that our body is composed of dancing photons.

TIME TRAVEL TEACHINGS

Wherever we are, whatever the condition, it is the best time to be alive.

SKYWALKER TEACHINGS

In these times we are each being reminded to awaken the wisdom eye of discernment, to observe, to not have any charge. Certainly you can direct the energy of the crystal. We were shown ways to make the water pure. I have even seen people return from the dead through sound and crystal. Everything we see, we test.

CRYSTAL TEACHINGS

From the sea of nothingness arises a sound, A-E-I-O-U — five tones, five winds, five breaths coming forth from the emptiness. Those simple sounds have a great significance for people from many traditions. They are related to sacred sounds practiced in the Kabbalah, African religions, old Christian chants, and Buddhist chants. That primordial sound means, from the circle of light-sound came five points, five rays of energy, much like the crow's foot. Just as everything in the universe reflects that one sound, that one light refracted into many forms, so in sitting with the crystal we again recognize the One, the essential unity within ourselves.

VOICES OF OUR ANCESTORS

Heart-to-heart, mind-to-mind communication acknowledging the sacred fiber that unites us all in this stream, is yet another foundation practice of magnetization. The gardener who cares for and respects the plants has the greatest harvest.

THE SEVEN WINDS

Each organ system in the body is resonating to a particular overtone that moves in a cycle, a pentatonic scale. Human nature relates to a cycle of five; the music of all ancient peoples has a pentatonic scale. The pentatonic scale is symmetrical, just as the beauty of our nature has an orderly form. There is a certain power in those intervals that we cannot speak about, but we can hear it. Our bodies and minds respond. We are the music, we are the sound, in that everything is vibration and vibration is consciousness. See the sound. Hear the light. Realize that which we are is constantly changing, constantly moving. Within that movement is a perfect stillness.

VOICES OF OUR ANCESTORS

The past is very much alive and the echoes contribute to the present.

LEARNING CHEROKEE WAYS

At this time it is said we are receiving energy from Canus Minor and this energy is coming into our galaxy at an angle, which is for change and quickening. We are being quickly reminded that we are part of a vast universe and that our actions reverberate through time and space. Also there are beings that live on other planets and other solar systems who are waiting for us to reach a harmonized group mind.

SKYWALKER TEACHINGS

Bio-resonance is a dance, just
as someone is dancing on the waterbed
and others begin to bounce, our thinking
contributes to the ripples in the field and the
appearances that arise. Extraordinary people
leave extraordinary waves of information
in the field. Those who have visited sacred
places surely have experienced this when
visiting Bodh Gaya, there is the sense
of wonder that one saw clearly that all
appearances are a dream and all are united
in this dance. That resounds continuously
through the environment and one who
approaches with curiosity will begin to
experience the significance of
seeking the ultimate truth.

MASTERFUL LIVING

*O*ften as people come closer and closer to understanding their true nature, they find themselves distracted and annoyed by things, or deep fears come up that they had not known were there. When these fears and other uncertainties of the mind arise, it is a great opportunity to see them as they are, just thought patterns, and have no attachment to them. Fear is an energy that can only be fed by itself. If the ignorant and hungry spirits have been feeding on you and they see that you are no longer going to generate the energy of confusion, they may make a lot of noise in your mind. Eventually, your mind realizes, yes, I have created this noise, I have created these hungry spirits, and I can sweep them out. It is all a process of change, of transformation, of refining transparency.

VOICES OF OUR ANCESTOR

*In each domain or realm there
exists their own physics.*

MASTERFUL LIVING

———

𝒰nderstanding ourselves
as multidimensional beings is expressed
through the Wind. The movement of the
Wind—up, down, or across—expresses
how potential takes form and how our
minds are part of a dynamic dance with
the atmosphere and the stars above. The
internal, external, and even the cosmic Winds
that can be perceived as a turning cross at
a black hole, are a reminder of an ongoing
process from whence even the most minute
expression is inseparable. These Winds
are a spiraling pathway through which
life's potential arises as form.

THE SEVEN WINDS

Why visualize? Visualization sets a clear path for the mind to recognize its potential. Visualization trains the mind that we may recognize the communication that is continually arising from all beings. Each person has been gifted with a mind, and this mind and view are part of a dynamic dance. Most importantly your sound, the quality of your being, is your thinking. This is a part of a great song and every human being is important in the fabric of humanity and in the fabric of our universe.

SKYWALKER TEACHINGS

May the wisdom seed in every being flourish and grow. Where there is the sound of war let there arise the sounds of mediation and reconciliation. Where there is confusion let it be unwound that the wisdom within each situation is revealed.

May there be joy, joy, and more joy.

MASTERFUL LIVING

The sun is exploring itself, going deeper to the core of its knowledge and that primordial state from whence it arose. The sun's self examination is a reminder to examine the nature of mind.

MEDICINE WHEEL MANDALA

In the first stage of doing
the dance together, we would experience
spiraling energy ascending and descending
within our bodies. At the same time, our
awareness of ourselves in a sphere of threads
of light surrounding us would expand and
make apparent the connections to other
beings in both the immediate environment
and those far, far away. Sometimes, we could
actually see other people and feel how, in
their own spiraling life force, their essence
still flowed with us. In this way, our ancestors
were shown to be very much like our own
physical form. Their wisdom of experience
was also accessible to us.

LEARNING CHEROKEE WAYS

*O*ur education continued to include exercises, which were helpful in tracking the little globules of light essences. I called them light trails left by people's minds and essences. The physical trail left by the body had a blue-gray luminescence that related to the physical health of that person. The emotions and thoughts would leave bubbles or holographic pictures as they passed through space. These holographic pictures contained the feeling, the experience, and the smell of those who had passed through the area.

LEARNING CHEROKEE WAYS

Our breath is connected
to the pulse beat of the universe.

GADUGI TEACHINGS

There is incredible power in understanding the sacred geometry of water and the energy of light. All of this is best supported and energized by empathy. What is empathy? Empathy is recognition that one electron recognizes another. Empathy is understanding that we are in a field and if one in the field is disturbed then others are disturbed. Empathy is truly healing. Empathy is more a non-conceptual state of awareness than compassion. Compassion is something that people cultivate and develop. The same way as we have reflexes, empathy in a well-tuned nervous system is sub-vocal.

TEACHING OF THE TREES

*When you drink water, make a prayer
for the water to become medicine.*

WATER TEACHINGS

Remember your natural state is luminosity, observe the clear quartz crystal, and let it be a reminder of the clarity of your wisdom eye.

CRYSTAL TEACHINGS

Observe the dance of the Holy Mother. Notice how the wind comes from the North. The wind's green breath nurtures the liver and the mind's ability to synthesize. We synthesize information from experience. May the eyes be clear so that we see the pathway of thoughts and synthesize information from experience, becoming a vortex. This vortex gives rise to one's physical form.

VAJRA DAKINI TEACHINGS

Without a spiritual foundation there can be no society.

VOICES OF OUR ANCESTORS

———

Ceremony marks cycles and creates the pathways for different energy flows to move. Ceremony is not just for one's personal experience. It is what one does to keep the experience and information from different realms integrated and it is an ongoing relationship.

LEARNING CHEROKEE WAYS

Through the breath, earth and
heaven meet; through the breath, we sense
the balance of Mother-Father within.

VOICES OF OUR ANCESTORS

The tree is an example of great compassion. It receives our breath and it returns to us life force energy through the wind. This energy is the breath of the Holy Mother's dance. In the wind of discursive thought, a wise practitioner observes the quiet of what is, so this green dancer, the green wind that gives rise to the liver and its ability to synthesize, reveals how the mind's projection can cause harm to the natural, pristine wisdom state. Offering apology to the Holy Mother, offering apology to the Buddha of the North, Amoghasiddhi, we recognize the gift of natural wisdom. The wind that stirs becomes the means of our exploration.

VAJRA DAKINI TEACHINGS

In our hearts we look to see divine presence. The crystal is the symbol of that perfection, which is within us.

VOICES OF OUR ANCESTORS

What is the significance of sound?
All appearances are vibration and the frequencies
of particular appearances signify that it is a color.
Our body, even our organs, has particular sounds.
When one is chanting, one is able to restore the
organ systems again to their proper, pristine tone.
Why? Because all appearances are vibration and
by chanting seed syllables, those ancient sounds
which are actually invigorated to the limbic region
of the brain, those ancient sounds restore our inner
harmony. The sounds change over time and as
they move through different cultures. The sounds
resonate with the frequency of the place, the land,
and the people who are reciting the sounds. There
are five tones that our limbic region in the central
brain respond to and these five tones are sacred
seed syllables that relate to the five skandas
and the five organ systems.

VAJRA DAKINI TEACHINGS

Our sacred power is our prayer power and the clarity of our thinking.

VOICES OF OUR ANCESTORS

The means of perceiving the nature of one's mind—to observe one's thoughts and actions—is to set the intention to be the best person one can possibly be, to benefit all.

THE SEVEN WINDS

The Medicine Wheel is a physical representation of the dynamic process of universes arising and the ongoing communication with that original pulse of wisdom from whence we are inseparable.

THE SEVEN WINDS

*L*et us not run from ourselves and not chastise, just make correction. Apologize to the wisdom being you are for any moments of forgetfulness and quicken your commitment to actualize that wisdom potential.

MASTERFUL LIVING

Basically, one human being is not just one human being. There are consciousnesses that live within you. Some are negative energy patterns. Mostly, they are the seeds of life that are consciousness explorers with you. Your body/mind is a canoe and you are exploring the field of potential. We have all made a promise, when we separated, that we would return the information to the field. Even the atoms within us are conscious.

MASTERFUL LIVING

What is spiritual sovereignty? It is the memory that we each have direct access to that seed of most awakened mind, that we have never been separated from it.

TEACHING OF THE TREES

Just as the tree receives sustenance from the earth and from the sky and offers the life giving energy of oxygen to the air, we receive and rejoice in our offering of appreciation to all those who support us. By cascading waves of grace and spiraling tendrils of light, our appreciation reaches those who have been kind to us and those who have not; all those who contributed to our deepening of understanding.

TEACHING OF THE TREES

Guru Padmasambhava made a
promise and commitment that certain things
would occur for whoever recites his mantra.
They will experience a change in whatever
is ailing them, whatever appears as an
obscuration, illusion, and any poison that
gives rise to suffering will be transformed.
The mantra, even the short version,
**OM AH HUNG VAJRA GURU PADMA
SIDDHI HUNG**, said in any moment
can unravel what appears as confusion.

VAJRA DAKINI TEACHINGS

By supporting grace and ease within the human condition, you also are supporting the transformation of polluted states in the earth.

MEDICINE WHEEL MANDALA

———

𝓡adiating outward from the crystal matrix are subtle shells of energy (worlds). The lunar and solar currents (descending and ascending spirals) of the wind plates correspond to such currents within the spine. The crystal matrix emits the basic pulse, the will to be, as encoded in DNA form, actualizing and maintaining the basic relationship of form potential. Earth, human, and solar processes are interwoven through this vibrational network. Hence, earth and human beings are ever in a reciprocal bio-resonant relationship. Awakened minds perceive clearly the relationship of energy pathways of individual mind and environment.

VOICES OF OUR ANCESTORS

May this water become a
medicine that washes away sorrow,
May it nurture the wisdom potential in all the people,
May this water, as it passes through my body,
May it arise as a vapor to clarify the emotions,
May the water be medicine for all beings,
May it know my appreciation,
May it carry the message of my appreciation
To all its forms and into all realms.

WATER TEACHINGS
Water Offering Prayer

Anger can become discriminating wisdom. Anger can also destroy the body, the health. What is the antidote? First, being appreciative, "Okay I have this life. I have awareness of this mind and these projections. Let me see beyond its conditioning."

MASTERFUL LIVING

*We choose a family wherein our
gifts may flourish, through which we can
complete a cycle of learning.*

VOICES OF OUR ANCESTORS

Like an onion, many worlds are enfolded, one within another. We have a choice about which frame we relate to.

LEARNING CHEROKEE WAYS

The emotions are energy and they
have arisen from what is wise and good. It's
only that we have forgotten this so when only
one part of the emotion is revealed, it becomes
like an anchor or a chain keeping one
in a pattern of repetition.

MASTERFUL LIVING

*K*now your breath is part of a dynamic dance. Through the breath and the glands, we return to the universe that which can be a lifeline and a lifesaver, drawing someone to the shore, free from illusion.

CRYSTAL TEACHINGS

The crystal is a living being, vibrating faster than the speed of light. It is not a solid; it is sound, ether, concretized. The crystal is a conscious being that has taken a particular form to resonate the basic sound of creation. The clear quartz crystal is one of the deeper mysteries of the practice of the Tsalagi people. With the quartz crystal one walks in all dimensions. It is also a key to healing, amplifying the proper tone so that the body may realize its resonance with the sound of creation.

VOICES OF OUR ANCESTORS

Our planet is expanding and
so is our consciousness.

MASTERFUL LIVING

The Holy Mother of the fire reminds us that nothing is ever the same transformation. Continuously, she transmutes and transforms. You then understand the importance of letting anger and rage dissolve into the love that accepts all beings as they are. Holy Mother, Holy Father, your dynamic dance reveals the fire that transforms and liberates. For this we are thankful,
for the gifts of life.

VAJRA DAKINI TEACHINGS

*L*et the blue flame reveal the purpose of our birth and the gifts we bring. Our commitment to share and explore is revealed in the rising of the blue flame. It joins with the rose flame, revealing the sacred dance of love and the power of inclusiveness; seeing all beings as our relatives in the Dance. The gold flame reveals clear intelligence, clear insight, penetrating beyond illusion of them and us, revealing we are all one in the field of mind.

CRYSTAL TEACHINGS

See in every being a hero. Understand that the Buddha, that the Christ-mind, is a seed within every being. Honor it wherever you go. Where there is discursive thought giving rise to separation, let us remember the power of sound and invite the sound to be the inspiration to dispel illusion.

VAJRA DAKINI TEACHINGS

When dancing, one expresses the
formation of matter and the inseparability
from the original pulse that gives
rise to all forms.

LEARNING CHEROKEE WAYS

Just as the crystal is awakened by pressure, sound, and movement, the seed of light within each one's heart awakens, too, when there is a conviction to understand.

THE SEVEN WINDS

You can use a mantra as an affirmation. Generally speaking, a mantra is composed of seed syllables that are originating sounds that arise from the vibrating field of Alaya. When they touch your heart, they reveal its point of understanding and then they have potency.

VAJRA DAKINI TEACHINGS

We were taught it is better to leave good information and as we walked, to give appreciation, listen, and honor the different types of beings, the environment, and the space we were walking through. The echoes of people's tears are like dust or mist floating in the environment, or something sticky upon the objects they once touched. Sometimes, even the environment can feel sticky. Other times, there is a sense of globules of energy, almost like emotional perspiration that is left in the wake of people moving through space. The past is very much alive and those echoes contribute to the present.

LEARNING CHEROKEE WAYS

The awakened beings are a
template that moves within each of us.

MASTERFUL LIVING

𝓐rgon is an element that does not change. It is said to be inert and when we take a breath in, we may be taking in the very molecules that were exhaled by some awakened being, whether we say it was Christ, or Buddha, Allah, or Mohammed. The circle of our breath connects us with the circle of the universe.

MASTERFUL LIVING

I dedicate the merit earned from this and all lives to the attainment of Buddha-mind and the release of all sentient beings from suffering.

DEDICATION

The Venerable Dhyani Ywahoo is Chief of the Wild Potato Clan of the Green Mountain Ani Yun Wiwa and the twenty-seventh generation holder of the ancestral Ywahoo lineage in the Tsalagi/Cherokee tradition. She is also a well-respected teacher of Vajrayana in the Drikung Kagyu and Nyingma traditions of Tibetan Buddhism. She founded the Vajradakini Nunnery, the first of its kind in North America and is Founder and Spiritual Director of Sunray Meditation Society, an international spiritual organization dedicated to world peace and reconciliation. Venerable is also the Founder of Sunray Peace Village in Lincoln, Vermont, a sanctuary based upon the Cherokee Peace Villages, and the Sunray Peace Village Land Trust, a conservation trust for prayer and ceremony in perpetuity. In 1990, Sunray was granted NGO status by the United Nations.

Her many books, music recordings, teachings, and information about upcoming workshops and seminars can be found through Beautyway Productions

www.beautywayproductions.com

www.sunray.org

Originally printed & hand bound by
Hudson River Bindery
for the 2011 Elder's Gathering

Book design by Write On The Wind.
Cover photo by Shan Watters.

Made in the USA
Charleston, SC
27 April 2012